CW00456088

NEW NAZARETHS IN US

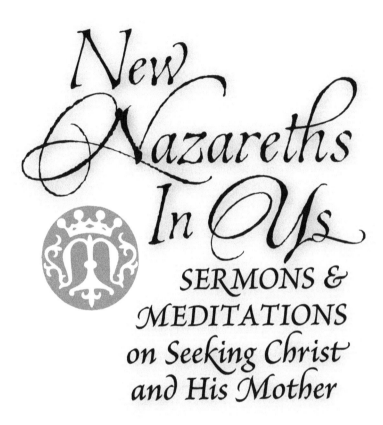

New Nazareths In Us

SERMONS & MEDITATIONS on Seeking Christ and His Mother

FATHER RYAN T SLIWA

THE CENACLE PRESS
AT SILVERSTREAM PRIORY

Unless otherwise noted, all scripture quotations
are from the Douay Rheims version

Quotations from St Thomas are taken from:
St Thomas Aquinas: Summa Theologica, translated
by the Fathers of the English Dominican Province
(Benzinger Brothers: New York, 1948).

Translations of Breviary and Missal texts are the author's own.

Nihil Obstat: Very Reverend Mark S. Stelzer, STD,
Censor librorum
Imprimatur: Most Reverend William Draper Byrne,
Bishop of Springfield
Springfield, 6th September, 2022

The Cenacle Press at Silverstream Priory
Silverstream Priory
Stamullen, County Meath, K32 T189, Ireland
www.cenaclepress.com

paperback 978-1-7396241-4-9
ebook 978-1-7396241-5-6

Book and cover design
by Michael Schrauzer

It has seemed good to your Highness that I should send you these prayers, which I edited at the request of several brothers. Some of them are not appropriate to you, but I want to send them all, so that if you like them you may be able to compose others after their example. They are arranged so that by reading them the mind may be stirred up either to the love or fear of God, or to a consideration of both . . .

[St Anselm of Canterbury,
Letter to the Countess Mathilda of Tuscany*]

---

* *The Prayers and Meditations of St Anselm*, trans Benedicta Ward (Penguin Books, 1973), 90.

CONTENTS

AUTHOR'S PREFACE

WHEN THE PRIEST ascends the pulpit to preach, he undertakes an impossibility. Somehow, he must speak of the ineffable. Somehow, he must move the human heart to act and to love. And as he does this, somehow he must disappear in the presence of the Word 'which enlighteneth every man that cometh into this world.' Yes, humiliatingly impossible.

And yet the priest is duty-bound to make his attempts. He knows that the grace of Holy Orders equips him. He knows that his liturgical and personal prayer, however fumbling, will cultivate in him a savour for the sacred. He knows that the Holy Ghost breathes in both himself and his hearers, and no word will be void.

The author of these pastoral writings feels both the weight and the wonder of all this, and these pages are his dutiful attempts.

What is the reader to find here? Speaking generally, he will not find controversy, in the precise sense of the word, nor even material strictly catechetical. Such things can be found readily by anyone who looks for them. What the reader will find (please God) is a liturgical look at the revealed mysteries. The sacred liturgy is the purest school of learning and sanctity for the faithful—when we contemplate it effectually, we flourish.

There are two types of writings in this book: sermons and meditations. The liturgical context of the sermons, with one or two exceptions, is the *usus antiquior* of the Roman Rite. In one way or another, they take as their subject the Mother of God.

As for the meditations, they are the work of imitation. In 1951, Msgr Ronald Knox published what he called 'Lightning Meditations.' He writes,

> It has been the custom to leave the man at the whetstone plenty of elbow room; and even in these more strenuous days we do not find fault with a sermon if it is on the right side of twenty minutes . . . Many of these lightning meditations (if I may give them that name) were written during the War, when one's friends seemed to need comfort rather than admonition. We still need comfort, and may yet need it more: let us have the oil and wine of the Samaritan.*

Since then, of course, the acceptable length of a sermon has been halved. But the point is that Knox's lightning meditations are meant to strike briefly but powerfully, with an eye to encouraging absent and beleaguered friends.—What priest today can fail to sympathise with such a work? Moreover, *meditation* is a key word. We are dealing, not with a legal brief or a position paper, but with relaxed, and yet reasoned, out-loud thinking. A meditation never pretends to be the last sayable word about anything. And the onus is on the reader—he

---

* *Stimuli,* Ronald Knox (Sheed and Ward: New York, 1951), vii-viii.

must do his own thinking, teasing out for himself whatever true things may be waiting beneath the limitations of the written word.

In May of 1883, preparing for his next academic post, Fr Gerard Hopkins wrote a poem in rhyming couplets: 'The Blessed Virgin compared to the Air we Breathe.' I draw the title of this volume from that poem:

> Of her flesh he took flesh:
> He does take fresh and fresh,
> Though much the mystery how,
> Not flesh but spirit now
> And makes, O marvellous!
> New Nazareths in us,
> Where she shall yet conceive
> Him, morning, noon, and eve.

It is true that the priest is always begging God to make up for his deficiencies; I do the same with regard to this little book. The point is that we should, somehow, become new Nazareths. All the rest is practically nothing.

25 March 2022

MEDITATION I

A World of What-ifs

IT HAS PERHAPS BEEN overstated, and by all sorts of people, that anxiety is a particularly distressing and universal phenomenon of human existence in our times. We might call it, with Julia Flyte, 'something absolutely modern and up-to-date that only this ghastly age could produce'.[1] And yet, even a cursory look around ourselves seems to confirm it. In one way or another, malaise and cynicism are all symptoms of a kind: so many disappointed hopes, so many thwarted hearts, so many good things either wounded or spoiled or lost. We say *what if?* so very often.

The cruelty is that when we say *what if* in our age, we are not usually daydreaming: the phrase is spoken often—far too often—with the taste of shame and bitterness. Anxiety and boredom may well be related, but anxiety makes a far greater demand on us than boredom and asserts itself more rudely and painfully. And there is nothing the least bit harmless about it.

1 Evelyn Waugh, *Brideshead Revisited* (Little, Brown, & Co: Boston, 1945), 200.

But in the face of anxiety, it might well be worth asking another sort of *what-if?*—*What if it were all true?* We mean: what if the basic Catholic propositions were true: that God himself, who created all things good, became truly man in the womb of the Virgin, made the expiating sacrifice upon the Cross, rose again, and who yet remains truly and unfiguratively present to the faithful in the Sacraments and in His Church, etc? What if the saints whose companionship we invoke, the mysteries we preach, and the morality we live were all perfectly real and had nothing of the contrived and fake character that many associate with formality and truth claims? And what if—most controversially—all this could really make the human heart ordered and happy in a way nothing else possibly could?

What if we gave all that a fair hearing? Think well on it. What if it were all true?

Go Forth, Daughters of Sion

A SERMON ON
THE QUEEN OF MAY

CATHOLICS FIND themselves in a spiritually precarious state whenever their worship is disrupted.[2] The enemy of our souls is undoubtedly pleased with the situation. On one level, this is true on account of the disagreement and confusion surrounding the question of *whether* our worship ought to have been disrupted in the first place. Such confusion is quite exploitable.

But there is more to the picture as well. The father of lies, the murderer from the beginning,[3] can move more freely where sacramental grace is absent. Now, he cannot win in the end—there is no thwarting Divine Providence—but his ferocity is proportionate to the shortness of his time.[4] All this comes to mind as we enter the fair month of May, in many places the customary time of First Communions and Confirmations and Ordinations. It is not too dire to say that we enter an impoverished springtime.

---

2   This sermon was composed during the lockdowns of the spring of 2020.   3   Cf John 8, 44.   4   Cf Revelation 12, 12.

All that is to speak of the Church's Sacraments. But we are met with another disruption of traditional piety: May devotions in honour of the Mother of God. We can safely speculate that the enemy is pleased about this as well.

To some, this observation will seem trivial or perhaps even appalling, given the various hardships that many are undergoing. But no, indeed—to call attention to the stoppage of our May devotions is not to trivialise, but to relativize: 'for our wrestling is not against flesh and blood; but against principalities and powers, against the rulers of the world of this darkness, against the spirits of wickedness in the high places.'[5]

Catholics know by a sacred instinct that the opening days of spring ought to witness the spontaneous and public outpouring of veneration and gratitude toward the Virgin Mary, who the Church honours with innumerable titles. But dark days require a redoubling of our devotion, not a stifling of it.

There is a Mass formulary that honours Mary under the titles of *Queen of All Saints and the Mother of Fair Love.*[6] Most of the texts are taken from the Wisdom Literature, and rightly so: the Immaculate Virgin is lady wisdom personified. Witness an excerpt from the epistle of the Mass:

> I have stretched out my branches as the terebinth: and my branches are of honour and riches.... I am the mother of fair love, and of fear,

---

5 Ephesians 6, 12.
6 This Mass exists in both the Missal of 1962 and in the reformed Missal of 1970.

and of knowledge, and of holy hope. In me is
all grace of the way and of the truth: in me is
all hope of life and of virtue.[7]

The same Mass begins with a text of special note.
The compiler of the Mass, acting under the liberty
of the Holy Ghost,[8] appropriates and modifies a few
verses from the Song of Songs: 'Go forth, daughters
of Sion, and see your Queen, whom the stars of morning praise: of whose beauty the sun and moon stand
in wonder, and on account of whom the sons of God
sing joyful songs.'[9]

The biblical text does not reference a queen, but
rather a king: King Solomon. But the modification is
entirely fitting; it is a song for the Queen of May.

Catholics must continue to go forth to see and to
meet their Queen, and this no matter the circumstances.
For the Queen Mother merits the praises of the very
cosmos. Our Mass introit tells us so. Not only do the
daughters of men give veneration to the great Queen,
but even the most beautiful elements of creation: the
stars, sun, and moon. This is indeed the truest moti-
vation for our May devotions. The very freshness and
beauty of the earth demand it.

Amidst our circumstances, it would not be out of
place for Catholics to experience a disquieting desire
for May devotions. For such a desire can inspire love.

---

7   Ecclesiasticus 24, 22, 24-25.
8   2 Corinthians 3, 17. 'Now the Lord is a Spirit. And where
the Spirit of the Lord is, there is liberty.'
9   Cf Song of Songs 3, 11. *Egredimini et videte, filiæ Sion, Reginam
vestram, quam laudant astra matutina: cujus pulchritudinem sol et
luna mirantur et jubilant omnes filii Dei.*

But what, then, is to be done? It would seem very little. But, in point of fact, it would be no small thing for us to speak our *Ave Marias* with greater fervour as a way to compensate for the disruption of our customary Marian devotions. Far be it from us to give Satan the satisfaction of seeing the praises of the Queen of May fall into neglect.

Cujus pulchritudinem sol et luna mirantur. The procession of the sun across the ecliptic that gives us our year and its seasons; its rise and fall which brings us from night to day—such beautiful and ceaseless regularity! And yet the Hail Mary, too, never stops. It is probably no exaggeration to say that it is the most frequently repeated prayer on the planet. How could man not wish to add his voice, weak and halting though it be, to the unceasing murmur of prayer that is at every hour rising from earth to heaven? The globe is never without the echo of the names of Jesus and Mary. And it is the Hail Mary that makes it so.

From the greatest to the least of us, we each have our praises to give. Thus in the summer of 1916, in the very midst of the Great War, Raïssa Maritain could write of our Lady with all truth: 'She is the calm lake of celestial Peace; the very pure mirror of the eternal Light; the white, sweet-scented rose on the breast of the benign Trinity.'[10]

---

10 *The Journal of Raïssa Maritain*, (Providence, Rhode Island: Cluny Media, 2020), 18. Entry of July 2nd, 1916. The Battle of the Somme began the day before.

MEDITATION II

Regarding Cheer

GOOD CHEER MAKES us friends of the angels and saints. They see all things *sub specie æternitatis*; and with that perspective very few things are of great importance. Such as we can, we do well to adopt the same outlook: because to be angry and lachrymose over what amounts to little is merely proof of how small we can be. It is an erroneous or unbalanced view of what truly matters that makes a man cheerless: for he can neither laugh at petty inconveniences, nor gracefully accept his own weakness, without undermining his sense of self-importance. Ultimately (and unhappily) he has placed himself rather high on the hierarchy of important things.

On the other hand, cheer makes a man great-hearted, because his eyes are looking toward eternity, where the most lasting and true things are. He knows what matters—namely, the things of God—and he makes no pretence of being more than what he is. So he may laugh at his own blunders and at the absurd pomps of the world around him. And this cheer makes him wear the world lightly. That is the foolishness for Christ spoken of by St Paul.[11]

Therefore, and contrary to what we might be inclined to think, cheer and good humour may not be primarily attached to joy. Rather, more fundamentally, *humility* makes a man cheerful because, once again, the humble man sees himself for what he is. Thus he is adept at evaluating the rest of what goes on around him accordingly. And, as we have already said, much of what does go on around him is comical because of the false pretences that are usually involved.

This sheds light, too, upon the Beatitude which says the poor in spirit are heirs to the earth. For the proud cannot turn aside from themselves; they have no time to inherit the good things promised to those who are humble enough to receive. So the saints go cheerfully to God, taught by the angels who are consumed with His glory.

---

11 Cf 1 Corinthians 4, 10.

Another Sort of Pharisee

OR THOSE WHO HAVE a singularly sweet conception of who Jesus Christ is—especially in his relationships with other human beings—chapter eleven of St Luke's Gospel presents a certain challenge. Our Lord's invectives against the Pharisees and scholars of Mosaic law are especially stinging. The first thing for us to remember is that, to be sure, the woes which he pronounces against them are movements of love. Not every illness needs the same treatment; not every soul needs the same formation. Christ the Physician adapts to the needs of each. It just so happens that the religious professionals of Israel needed some stiff remedies.

One of the woes pronounced by Our Lord is of special interest: 'Woe to you who build the monuments of the prophets; and your fathers killed them'.[12]

Here, the wild inconsistency of the religious climate is pointed out. Past generations slew the prophets out of murderous indocility; future generations, however,

---

12   Luke 11, 47.

admire these same prophets, without any spiritual conversion having taken place in the meantime. For his part, Jesus Christ is in the same line of the prophets: but he earns no admiration and obedience from those who ought to have been the first to understand and to obey.

There is a similar kind of pharisaism at work in our times among Catholics. We are speaking of the souls who were baptised as infants and who passed through the *cursus* of Catholic education; they were reared in families who have been Catholics for generations, and they are quick to make a boast of these credentials. And yet, they hold moral or doctrinal positions that are fundamentally at odds with perennial Catholic teaching. The phenomenon is easily explainable; but we do well to see it for what it is: another sort of pharisaism.

Such people do not often critically evaluate what they believe or how they live. It is enough for them to believe that the adjective *Catholic* can be appended to their identities. But they are in the same tradition as the Pharisees. As St Luke records, the Pharisees could not see the fundamental inconsistency of their religious posture. Thus, the same pattern is repeated in our time.

Sic Deus Dilexit Mundum

A SERMON FOR WHIT MONDAY

'Thus God loved the world, such that
he gave his only son' (*John 3, 16*).[13]

ODAY'S BENEDIC-
tus antiphon puts the mys-
tery before us: the primacy of divine charity. Which is
to say that the Father sent the Son *out of love* for the
world, 'so that all who believe in him might not perish,
but have eternal life.' Divine Providence is, ultimately,
a work of love. The baptised understand this. They may
need the occasional reminding; they always need to live
distinctly holy lives in order for this love to take hold of
them: but that God is love and that he works all things
for a loving purpose is not a novel doctrine.

However, for many souls—can we say, for *most?*—the
truth of a loving Providence is not necessarily one of
life's givens. It is no enigma to see why, in view of the
mortal troubles that can afflict the human family. But
in fact the antiphon presumes this: 'God so loved the
world ... so that those who believe in him *may not perish.*'
Ut non pereant. It is as Yeats wrote:

---

13 Author's own translation.

Things fall apart; the centre cannot hold;
Mere anarchy is loosed upon the world,
The blood-dimmed tide is loosed, and everywhere
The ceremony of innocence is drowned;
The best lack all conviction, while the worst
Are full of passionate intensity.[14]

The sacred liturgy is always profoundly realistic. Thus today we stand in the midst of both a sea of human ills and the mystery of Pentecost. We ought to think of some mysterious words which Our Lord spoke at the last supper regarding the Holy Ghost:

> And yet I can say truly that it is better for you I should go away; he who is to befriend you will not come unless I do go, but if only I make my way there, I will send him to you. He will come, and it will be for him to prove the world wrong, about sin, and about rightness of heart, and about judging. About sin; they have not found belief in me.[15]

Mysterious that the Holy Ghost should come in order to convict the world of its wrongness. But this is not some literary expression of the intolerance of Christians: the Holy Ghost convinces man of his wrongness and sin precisely so as to move him in the other direction. This explains the prophetic mission of the Church (and, by extension, the prophetic *munus* of the holy priesthood). Indeed, it is part of the logic of love to speak of error and danger, and the grace of Pentecost comes burning with this grace. We have only to study the preaching of the Apostles immediately after Pentecost to see this truth at work.

---

14   W B Yeats, 'The Second Coming,' lines 3-8.
15   John 16, 7-9 (Knox).

There is also a Marian component hidden in our text. 'God so loved the world that *he gave* his only begotten Son.' Christ the Lord did not simply appear spontaneously and spectre-like in human history: he was prepared for and *given*. Our Lady, to put it this way, provides for the given-ness of Jesus Christ. His coming is so complete and real that he took flesh of the Virgin Mary. The Christmas mysteries celebrate this particularly, and we are reminded of it here during the octave of Pentecost. Entirely fitting that we should be: for it was by the power of the same Holy Ghost that the Incarnation took place.[16]

A number of conclusions emerge. First, that the Catholic should recognize his glorious strangeness. He knows that charity is the ultimate thing. Despite all that may obscure the matter, the truth remains the same: in God all things work together for love. *Sic Deus dilexit mundum.* And the Catholic casts his hope on that. *This ultimate charity can receive and support every one of his pains and perplexities.* But it is a doctrine he must live courageously, because much of the world thinks him a fool for holding it. Yet it is why the Church may sing *Alleluia* so frequently. The Church's *Alleluia* is not simply a liturgical nicety, but a little Credo about what is—it contains a world of shining metaphysics. *Sic Deus dilexit mundum.*

Second, therefore, to live outside of Christ's influence—indeed, to live outside of his Church—is not a safe place for the human being to be. For there is no benign, neutral state in which man may hope to eke out a safe and comfortable interim as he waits for death. Man either lives or perishes. But this dire truth makes

---

16   Luke 1, 35.

the charity of God to flame out all the more clearly, for an entire system of means has been given for man's benefit. That system of means is the Church. He has only to be humble enough to believe and submit to the work of grace.

Third, an august Queen presides in the light of this drama of charity. Concretely, this is the theological foundation of all authentic Marian apparitions—in our times, Lourdes and Fatima deserve special note. It is not without reason that she bears the titles *Seat of Wisdom, House of Gold, Ark of the Covenant*, and *Gate of Heaven*. Seat, house, ark, gate. And it is precisely this reason why it is fitting that we should have learned at Fatima that the Father desires to establish devotion to the Immaculate Heart of Mary, for it is only to draw souls back to a work that he has already accomplished: *Sic Deus dilexit mundum ut Filium suum unigenitum daret.* Little wonder that the Holy Ghost inspires the faithful never to forget this. In trouble and in happiness, ours it is to linger by the Virgin of Pentecost.

MEDITATION IV

The Scandal of Weeds

*I*N THE WAKE OF scandal, it is true that we live in a time and place where the moral authority of the Church is severely weakened. But as soon as we admit that, we are also obliged to be clear about what scandal actually is. Disapproving of or feeling morally outraged by something is not scandal; that is something else. No, taking issue is not the same as taking scandal. To put it most succinctly, giving scandal is to act or fail to act in such a way as to lead another into serious sin.[17] It is to put an obstacle—a *skandalon*—in the way of another's attainment of the good.

Nevertheless, scandal given or taken cannot quite be the last word, for we have Christ's parable of the Weeds and the Wheat to reckon with: 'And his men asked him, Wouldst thou then have us go and gather them up? But he said, No; or perhaps while you are gathering the tares you will root up the wheat with them. Leave them to grow side by side till harvest.'[18]

---

17   Cf *The Catechism of the Catholic Church*, nn 2284, 2236.
18   Matthew 13, 29-30.

The experienced gardener knows all about weeds. Certainly the purpose of a seedbed is not to grow weeds, but to grow flowers and crops and herbs. And yet that same gardener is not shocked—and certainly not scandalised—when the weeds appear. The weeds are undesirable and must be removed; their growth will, eventually, sap and crowd the soil; they are unattractive to behold; they are simply not the point of a garden. But in the presence of weeds, the flowers do not instantly lose their bloom nor the fruits their sweetness; the whole thing does not have to be uprooted; there is a harvest on the way to put everything in order.

It is well worth noting, too, who are the actors in the parable: it is the gardener and his servants and the enemy, that is, God and his angels and Satan. The wheat (understandably enough) doesn't even have a speaking part in this parable, let alone the free agency to do any landscaping of its own.

Scandal given is a tragedy; there is nothing frivolous about it. But it must not be taken as the last word either—though a certain worldly spirit often does this. In much the same way as the gardener does not fear the weeds, souls must not fear the presence of evil characters in the Church or elsewhere. 'An enemy has done this.' (Besides, we each have sins enough to keep our compunction well occupied.) *But it has been foreseen.*—Christ has already warned us that it would be so. When the weeping Saint Mary Magdalene mistook Christ for the gardener, she was not altogether wrong. Christ is the Divine Gardener, and see how faithful he is to us. The real integrity of the Church is not harmed;

the whole system is not invalidated; it does not need to be uprooted.

Had Christ *not* taught as he did, we might certainly wonder. However, this parable is a most vital proof text, and it is well that it should be kept very close to heart by anyone who would have a mature Catholic faith in the world today.

MEDITATION V

Corruptio Optimi

NFORTUNATELY, FEW Latin *dicta* are more helpful for interpreting reality than this. *Corruptio optimi pessima.* Indeed, the corruption of the best is the worst.

There is, all the same, a stark proportion to reality; and because the world is an ordered place—a *kosmos*—it must be so. This is not to say, however, that what is best depends upon what is worst in order to exist. Manichaeism was proven false a long time ago. And this is the first thing our little sentence teaches us: we are dealing with *corruption*, decay, deficit, darkening, a breaking down of something that ought to be otherwise—not the acknowledgement of some necessary opposite of goodness that is a thing unto itself. The darkness to which we refer here is always a *departure*, not a complement.

We are also in the territory of St Augustine's insight: that evil is a *privatio boni*, a privation of the good. What is good is the fundamental reality, not what is evil. Thus evil, on the other hand, has no form of its own; it is the shadowy space where a good ought to be.

Creation is *what is*. Revelation is *what is*. God himself is the bedazzling *I AM*, and all truth proceeds from him. Truth is The Best. If this can be grasped, it stands perfectly to reason that the more dramatic a departure from The Best, the more profound the worst becomes and appears. Thus we have no reason to be caught off guard. *Corruptio optimi pessima* is not an esoteric principle, something that only the clever and few can see: it turns out to be the purest common sense.

If all that be true, then are we not allowed at least some degree of serenity? There is peace to be had in the straightforward acknowledgement that something is wrong. Serenity is possible because The Best is the most real and lasting. A dramatic corruption still points to The Best from which it fell and decayed; otherwise, we would not know it to be the corruption it is. Thus, peace is possible because if some circumstance, or someone, has swerved from The Best, there is always hope for a return.

Coram Ipso Ministravi

A SERMON FOR
OUR LADY OF THE SNOWS

'And in the holy dwelling place I have
ministered before Him' (*Ecclesiasticus 24, 14*).

ODAY WE CELEBRATE the dedication of a church;
but our Mass texts are taken entirely from the Common
of Our Lady. More or less, we have a Saturday Ladymass.
And yet, this is hardly unfitting—quite the contrary.
To see just how fitting it is, we might fix our attention
especially on the epistle.[19] (Which text also appears in
the Little Office of Our Lady, and both the Roman and
monastic Divine Office).

The dedication of churches—from the humblest to
the greatest—calls to mind the mystery of God-with-us.
Every Catholic church is a sign of the presence and
activity of the Most High God, given perfect expression in the Incarnation of Jesus Christ. Similarly, *today's
epistle is filled with language that expresses the rootedness
of the Blessed Virgin Mary in salvation history and in the
Church: Ante sæcula creata sum,* 'before the ages I was

---

19 Ecclesiasticus 24, 14-16.

created'; *Non desinam*, 'I shall not cease to be'; *Firmata sum*, 'I have been established'; *In Ierusalem potestas mea*, 'My might is in Jerusalem'; *In civitate...radicavi*, 'In the city...I have taken root'; *In plenitudine sanctorum detentio mea*, 'My tarrying is in the fullness of the saints.'

The church whose dedication we celebrate today is old, not new: the first edifice on the site was constructed in the middle of the fourth century—that is, about the 350's. Naturally, however, this does not mean that devotion to the Mother of God took 350 years to arise in the Church. We just heard the words of sacred Scripture tell us so. *Ante sæcula creata sum. Firmata sum. In plenitudine sanctorum detentio mea.* No, the stones of the church give material expression to a devotion long held.

Now, within this church—which today we call St Mary Major—there is an ikon of the Virgin Mother: *Maria, Salus Populi Romani* Mary; 'Health,' or even 'Salvation of the Roman People.' The original form of the ikon is reputed to have been painted by St Luke himself on a table made by St Joseph and Our Lord. We know that St Gregory the Great received the ikon in Rome with great solemnity, and from that day onward the image enjoys a very storied history. The church itself, as we would expect, has undergone a number of renovations throughout the past millennium and a half.

But in this church the ikon is a powerful sign. The sacred author of Ecclesiasticus reports the words of the Immaculate Virgin: 'In the holy dwelling place I have ministered before Him.' Most profoundly, this refers to the place of the Immaculate One in the eternal designs of God: she ministered before him even before the divine plan was made manifest in creation. (Indeed, it is why we call the Immaculate Conception a *prevenient* grace.) But in the sacred ikon—figuratively but truly—the Virgin continues to minister before him. She continues to be the health of the Roman people in this holy habitation. Every authentic Marian apparition points to this same truth. The Virgin ministers before God on our behalf, according to the designs of his wonderful Providence.

'In the holy place I have ministered before Him.' This is the mystery we commemorate, and indeed venerate, today: namely, the Virgin's abiding ministration on our behalf. Surely the dark intelligences of God's enemies are never at rest; surely we in our weakness flag and fail.—But the Immaculate One is also constantly ministering before the Most High. She continually echoes her Magnificat before him, which is why the holy Church prays it each evening. Think well on it: the setting sun gives expression to the futility of relying on our own strength, which will always ebb; there is no hope for us, left to ourselves. But at just that moment, we take confidence and with child-like mimicry we say, *Magnificat anima mea Dominum.* 'My soul doth magnify the Lord!'

Dear friends, how noble a thing to declare our ancient and sacred love in our ancient and sacred tongue: *Sancta Maria, Salus Populi Romani: ora pro nobis!* May it never cease to fall from our lips and from our hearts.

MEDITATION VI

Worse Than Death

FOR THE CATHOLIC, there are indeed things worse than death. And by *death* here we mean death of the body. And at the first, it wants saying that death is a matter never to be spoken of lightly. For who among us has not mourned for our dead? (Sorrow, after all, springs from love.) And furthermore, who among us can be certain of our own dispositions when death comes for us? There is a reason why we speak of the grace of final perseverance. Who among us can be sure that we will encounter our last moments with courage and serenity? That is, if we will even be so fortunate as to be able to salute our death as it arrives. No, speaking of death can never be done with cocksure casualness.

All that being noted, there is something worse than the death of the body. But what exactly? Most profoundly, the moral compromise which we give the name *sin*. To sin is to act against our very selves, even as this or that sin may be against one's neighbour, or even against God himself. We become something we are not meant to be when we sin; a certain spiritual disintegration takes place within us. And if the sin is grievous, the soul is in a state of death even while the body lives on. This is why St John distinguishes between sin that leads *to death* and sin that does not. And he is not talking about death of the body.

Perhaps to some, all that sounds too much like rote catechizing. However, the French novelist and social critic Georges Bernanos has something interesting to say in this connection:

> No one who sees trouble coming can be sure of escaping it, but at least he can look it in the face, and then the trouble will not strike him shamefully in the back. For there is something worse than dying—it is to die deceived.[20]

In context, Bernanos is not speaking of personal sin; but he does confirm for us that, indeed, there is something worse than death. And yet, if we are correct (and honest) about the nature of sin, we see that it is a kind of deception, and grave sin a most acute deception, indeed, on a number of levels. To sin is to have chosen a false good instead of a true good. We go deceived, either by ourselves or the world or the fallen angels. In such a case, yes, it is the most acute of deceptions: for the body lives, but the soul is dead.

Surely, this is a heavy meditation, but there is hope to be met with: Christ the Lord, through his Church, offers himself as our unique remedy and safety.

But one last point. If all we have said is true, then our very lives depend upon reckoning with death. After

---

20   Georges Bernanos, *Liberty: the Last Essays*, trans Joan and Barry Ulanov (Providence, Rhode Island: Cluny Media, 2019), 194.

all, who among us would like to die deceived? And yet this is precisely what we prepare ourselves to do if we do not see—and with crystal clarity—what exactly we do to ourselves when we sin. If we begin to believe that *material* misfortune is the greatest evil to be avoided, then it is impossible for us to serve God in any real way, because death is merely the highest expression of material misfortune. But no, the Catholic soul is strong and lively only to the extent that he or she understands that there is most certainly something worse than death of the body.

MEDITATION VII

A Laborious Rest

HERE ARE WORDS of encouragement and comfort in the eleventh chapter of St Matthew's Gospel; we are familiar enough with the text:

> Come to me all you that labour and are burdened, and I will refresh you. Take up my yoke upon you, and learn of me, because I am meek, and humble of heart: And you shall find rest to your souls. For my yoke is sweet and my burden light[21].

But there is also something curious at work here.

We note that 'I will refresh you' is immediately followed by 'take up my yoke.' *Reficiam vos; tollite iugum.* A moment of whiplash, we might even say: our Lord goes from a promise of rest to a command to labour. *Which is it?* we might ask.

Well, both. Two kinds of labour are implied in our Lord's discourse: the sort that is burdensome and wearying, and the sort that refreshes. Our Lord is speaking

---

21 Matthew 11, 28-30.

to those who are already burdened with the first sort of burden; therefore, he means to give them another yoke—the second kind of burden—but one that will refresh instead. Thus, the human person can labour for Christ and be refreshed; or he may labour for everyone or everything else and remain burdened and worn down.

To repeat the point, if somewhat differently, we see that the very act of serving Christ is its own rest—perhaps difficult to acknowledge, but nevertheless true. But the matter is a rather essential one: for the Catholic way would be far more attractive to the world if each of us bore Christ's yoke more cheerfully. In the face of relentless suffering, it is no small thing to demonstrate that we are at rest, at home, with our divine service. Come what may, we ought to be at ease with our Catholic faith, even if it isn't always easy.

If something like the above were not true, then the alternative is simply to consign Christ's words to the realm of incoherence. For the believer, this is an impossibility. For the non-believer, however, the risk may be too great: a hopeless burden is all that really awaits him.

Of Chastity & Covered Shame

A SERMON FOR
THE ASSUMPTION

ALL SIN IS SHAMEFUL. Here, we could easily reflect upon the general place and purpose of shame in human life.[22] For now, however, suffice it to say, all sin is accompanied by shame—felt by us either openly or in some less-than-conscious way. Nevertheless, a particular sense of shame often attends sins against chastity. There are reasons for this, too, but which we leave aside for the moment. All the same, not only can this shame be poignant, but it can also be especially persistent, lingering on even after sins have been absolved by the Sacrament of Penance. And this is to say nothing of the psychological scars that can remain impressed upon the soul as well.

Yet we discover the theological origins of this shame in the opening chapters of Sacred Scripture: 'And the eyes of them both were opened: and when they perceived themselves to be naked, they sewed together fig leaves, and made themselves aprons.'[23]

---

22   One thinks, for instance, of the theme of holy shame in the anthropology of the late Alice von Hildebrand.
23   Genesis 3, 7.

Sins against chastity are especially apt to remind us of our fundamental nakedness before God. That is, violations of the Sixth and Ninth Commandments directly point to the dignity that was forfeited by our first parents—and, more immediately, they point to the personal continuation of that forfeiture by our own sins. Put in more precise theological terms, sins of unchastity make us to feel the loss of *integrity*: that is, the gift which Adam and Eve possessed whereby the faculties and passions worked together in harmonious action, unaffected by disordered concupiscence. They lost this gift on account of sin, and now all human beings must bear the burden of the loss. To be sure, now that his passions are in disarray, man is inclined to all manner of sin. But once again, it is unchastity that especially and mysteriously causes him particular difficulty and shame.

Over this sad tale, however, is the shining mystery of the Assumption of the Virgin Mary.

Today, the second nocturn of the Roman Breviary contains a sermon by St John Damascene (c. 675-749). He writes, 'Today, the Eden of the New Adam receives the living paradise in which the condemnation was broken, in which the Tree of Life was planted, in which our nakedness was covered.'[24]

Sins of unchastity leave man earth-bound and exposed. If such sins are habitual, man becomes in a manner obsessed and chained to pleasure. He cannot raise his eyes to higher things and to the heavenly places. On the contrary, all he sees is his own nakedness and

---

24 From *Oratio 2 de Dormitione BMV: Hodie Eden novi Adam paradisum suscipit animatum, in quo soluta est condemnatio, in quo plantatum est lignum vitæ, in quo operta fuit nostra nuditas.*

that of others. Yet Our Lady is taken up, beyond all the limitations of this life; beyond all that is base and tawdry. Likewise, under the action of grace, man is capable of transcending even his most shameful misdeeds. In Baptism, his very destiny is to rise above what may tempt him and sully his dignity. The Assumption bids him remember—bids him remember his dignity; bids him remember that *the mercy and Providence of God are sovereign*, not the moral and emotional wreckage that man often produces.

As the Damascene says, the Virgin Mary's Assumption covers the nakedness of Eve. Sins of unchastity are especially healed under the grace of the Assumption. Thus, shame never needs to have the last word. Little wonder, then, that the introit of today's Mass speaks of Our Lady being *clothed* with the sun. She bears no shame—but she is clothed in grace, and we are consumed with gratitude and hope because of it.

MEDITATION VIII

The Simplicity of the Word

FAMILIARITY, IT MUST be admitted, *does* make it difficult to appreciate the Gospels for the precious and remarkable things they are. And *things* is certainly not the right word to use. True enough that we may be familiar with certain passages—we have favourites; we more or less remember them when they come around each year. In this case, familiarity may not breed contempt, but something worse: complacence.

And yet, we ought to allow ourselves to be the struck by the directness and austerity of the Gospels. When it comes to narrative, clinical or movie-like detail may be more to our tastes. But this the Gospels do not give us. (Strunk and White might have approved.) We find a dramatic example in the fourteenth chapter of St Matthew:

> [A]nd looking up to heaven, he blessed, and brake, and gave the loaves to his disciples, and the disciples to the multitudes. And they did all eat, and were filled.[25]

---

25 Matthew 14, 19.

We are furnished with no details about how the miracle looked, no description of the mechanics, as it were. Did additional loves simply appear in baskets or in Our Lord's hands? Did more bread appear in the place where the loaves were broken? And what about the fishes? Moreover, we hear nothing about the reaction of the disciples or the bystanders. Unlike during other miracles, no words of astonishment are recorded, no protestations or incredulity, no declarations about the identity of Christ. We are told precious little.

To be sure, none of this is to point out a flaw in the way the Gospels were written. In fact, it is just the opposite—the austerity, directness, and simplicity of the style of the Gospels have something to tell us about the nature of the interior life.

Simplicity is always a destination toward which the soul ought to be tending: for the divine action is not complicated. It may be profound, subtle, hidden; but it is never complicated. Man, with his doubts and hesitations and stubbornness, is complicated; God is not. Little wonder, then, that the Evangelists should be inspired to compose in a style that mirrors the simplicity of God.

Thus, man ought *to hear* with simplicity—without hedging and qualifying. 'Unless you be converted, and become as little children . . .'[26]

A passage from Strunk and White may actually be fitting here:

> Vigorous writing is concise. A sentence should contain no unnecessary words, a paragraph no unnecessary sentences, for the same reason that

---

26   Matthew 18, 3.

a drawing should have no unnecessary lines and a machine no unnecessary parts. This requires not that the writer make all his sentences short, or that he avoid all detail and treat his subjects only in outline, but that every word tell.[27]

This is not to say that the Holy Ghost is concerned with using verbal economy—He needs no manual of style to convey the Word. But when He speaks, every word does *tell*. Ours, then, to have a spiritual life that is correspondingly vigorous and simple.

---

27 William Strunk and E B White, *The Elements of Style*, 4th ed (Macmillan Publishing Co, 2000), 12-13.

Terra Dedit Fructum Suum

A SERMON FOR THE IMMACULATE HEART OF MARY

'The earth has given its fruit' *(Psalm 66, 7)*.

S T JOHN EUDES REFERS to Our Lady as the earth.[28] He has warrant for doing this both from the Fathers and from the Scriptures. As far as the Sacred Scripture is concerned, today's epistle makes it quite clear: 'As a vine I bore a sweet aroma, and my flowers are the fruit of honour and riches.... Come over to me, all you that desire me, and be filled with my fruits.'[29]

(This same epistle, it is worth noting, is also used on the feast of Our Lady of Mt Carmel and on the Vigil of the Immaculate Conception. Thus, there is a theological tie that unites these three feasts—but that is for another time.)

It is out of the earth that all vines and fruits and flowers grow.

Then we can think of two texts from the Holy Gospels: the first, in which Our Lord speaks of the good

28 *The Admirable Heart of Mary* (P. J. Kenedy & Sons: 1948), Part Two, Chapter IV.   29 Ecclesiasticus 24; 23, 26.

earth receiving the seed to bear thirty, sixty, or a hundred fold;[30] and the second, in which, speaking of his Mother, he says: 'Yea rather, blessed are they who hear the word of God and keep it.'[31] These two texts—of the rich soil and obedience—are joined in Our Lady's Heart.

You know the custom of blessing blossoms and herbs on the feast of the Assumption, the octave day we are now celebrating. You know, too, that this custom is connected to the tradition of how the Apostles, at the time of Our Lady's Assumption, found her tomb empty of her body, yet filled with blossoms and greens. And yet, it is also true that this is just the time of year (as I recently learned) in which herbs are to be cut and dried. Thus the Church stands ready to bless the yield of the earth in the presence of the Immaculate One. *Terra dedit fructum suum.*

Which brings us to today's text. In the monastic office, Psalm 66 is prayed at the beginning of Lauds daily. It is a psalm that calls down the mercy of God, a mercy which is indeed new every morning.[32] It is a psalm of benediction and of praise. All these make it perfectly fitting for the Church's prayer as the sun begins to colour the sky in the east. But if what we have been saying is true, namely, that according to the language of Scripture the earth often refers to Our Lady, then Psalm 66 speaks of her, too: 'Let the peoples praise Thee, O God, let all the peoples praise Thee: the earth has given its fruit.'

Fruit represents all the divine benefits. And when Israel of the Old Dispensation is given material blessings—

---

30 Matthew 13, 18.   31 Luke 11, 28.

32 Lamentations 3, 22-23.

like rich harvests, fertility in marriage, rest from ene-mies—all these are so many prefigurements of the fruitfulness of grace. On account of the mystery of the divine maternity, the Immaculate One is the earth out of which springs the Word Incarnate. Which is why St Bonaventure could teach that 'all salvation springs from Mary's Heart.'[33]

Thus, Psalm 66 is a Marian psalm. *Terra dedit fructum suum.* We say it many times a day: 'And blessed is the fruit of thy womb, Jesus.' As the earth ripens toward the harvest, the Heart of Mary shines over the Church as the font of all spiritual harvests. Anywhere we see the fruitful earth—both in the Scriptures and even in nature itself—we see Mary.

Please God, we may begin, more and more, to see her everywhere.

---

33 *In Psalt. B. Virg.* Psalm 79.

The Problem of Patriotism

*T*O UNDERSTAND this problem we do well to understand what patriotism is. St Thomas puts it succinctly:

> The principles of our being and government are our parents and our country, and they have given us birth and nourishment. Consequently, man is a debtor chiefly to his parents and to his country, after God. Wherefore just as it belongs to religion to give worship to God, so does it belong to piety, in the second place, to give worship to one's parents and one's country.[34]

On account of our indebtedness, justice and worship conspire to give us piety; which, when we render it to our country and fellow citizens, is patriotism. And by 'worship' in this context, of course, we do not mean the *latria* which is due to God alone. Rather, 'piety is a protestation of the charity we bear towards our parents and country.'[35]

How noble a virtue is patriotism, then.

---

34 *STh* IIaIIæ, Q 101, art 1, res.   35 Ibid, art 3, ad 1.

But a difficulty emerges. What becomes of the virtue of piety when one realises there are rather acutely unlovable things about one's country? Whence piety when the fatherland shows signs of profound ill health? Are we indeed to show piety to a nation that countenances gravely unjust and even perverse laws? One thinks immediately of state-sponsored infanticide, for example.

As it turns out, the answer to the problem may come from an unlikely source: the cloister.

Out of the monastic culture of the West—which must mean that culture which was brought to birth under the Rule of St Benedict—out of this culture comes the following definition of what a monk is. That is, the monk is an *amator fratrum et loci*: a lover of the brethren and of the place. He loves the brethren with whom Divine Providence has joined him and he loves the very place in which Divine Providence has rooted him. And that brings us to a definition of patriotism as good as that of St Thomas'.

Man cannot love abstractions, because he is not only a soul. Thus, while it is true that the patriotic man must love immaterial goods—like law and the virtues which the law attempts to enshrine—it is also true that man loves such things *in concreto*. Love and the homage of service can only be rendered to the real, concrete persons right in front of us. And this is challenging enough. While it is true that I may not share or love the opinions of this or that of my fellow citizen, I may still love *him*. We love our neighbours because they are our neighbours, for good or ill. Patriotism has free play in such relationships.

All men live out the drama of life within peopled places: the objects of his 'protestation of charity' are therefore right in front of him. It is also part of patriotism to love the very land or neighbourhood or city in which one lives. Loving our *locum* is something we can do that hardly needs to be outright political, at least in the sense that we usually mean the word. Heaven help us, let there be nothing partisan about a mountain or shaded lane or a city park! For places matter. And, more often than not, we live in places of beauty that, if we stop to notice, are very worthy of our grateful love.

The man who loves his land and neighbour is a pious patriot. And if the laws or history or current state of health of his country disturb him—as in these troubled times they ought to disturb him—then perhaps a man can think of himself as a monk does. Whatever illusions the media may give, every man, woman, and child is cloistered: cloistered in a little place with a few brethren. If only these could be loved, and loved truly, we might be astonished at the result.

Benedicta Tu!

A SERMON FOR
THE BIRTHDAY OF MARY [36]

Blessed are you, holy Virgin Mary, deserving of all praise;
from you rose the Sun of Justice, Christ our God.

S O, THE VIRGIN MARY is real. In case there were any doubt. And so today is a big deal. It is a big deal because of the words I quoted a moment ago: indeed, Our Lady deserves all praise because she is the mother of Christ our God. What's more, all the mysteries of Mary are like a golden thread woven through history. And without this thread—without her—we would not have things as they now are. Might God have arranged things differently? Indeed. Only, he did not. And so our love of Mary is very simple, and don't let anyone convince you otherwise: 'Blessed are you, Virgin Mary, deserving of all praise; from you rose the Sun of Justice, Christ our God.'

But in order for Mary to be who she is, to have done what she did, and to do now what she continues to do, of

---

36   Preached on the 8th of September to high-school students.

course, first she had to be born. That is what we celebrate today—the beginning of a life so beautiful and great.

Remember that God's plan for history hangs together in a perfectly ordered way. The phrase we use to describe this plan is 'Divine Providence'. We may look around the world now and not see very much order and goodness, but believe me, it's there. God is not making it up along the way, and we're celebrating one of the high points of his plan right now; and nothing, however bad, can take it away. Blessed are you, holy Virgin Mary.

However, in just the same way, nothing can ever remove you or me from our place in Divine Providence. The proof is in the woman we are commemorating now. Today she is born; we see how she fits into the divine plan for human history; and, on account of her fidelity, everything was goodness and victory. You and I are not the Virgin Mary. But we were born; we are part of the same plan; and our lives can be all goodness and victory if we are faithful. We may not have a leading role in the drama of history, but we are actors in the same play; just because we may not be sitting in the first chair, that doesn't mean we aren't playing in the same symphony.

In light of all that, and by way of conclusion, three practical things occur to me to mention; three things that we ought to do. First, to realise that there is indeed a divine plan; that it is all goodness and nothing can derail it; and that we personally have a place in it. Second, Catholics ought to be especially skilled at rejoicing wherever they see God at work—either in themselves or in others. Everything that is good and pure gives us some little glimpse of the Virgin Mary, and we shall be happier and stronger in God if we begin to see Mary, however hidden, wherever we look. Third, we ought never to grow bored with marvelling at Mary. 'Blessed are you, holy Virgin Mary, deserving all praise!' When you find it hard to pray, simply tell God how wonderful the Virgin Mary is—the Lord Jesus never ignores a compliment toward his Mother.

Of Modernism & Mary

POPE ST PIUS X PRO-
mulgated his encyclical *Pas-
cendi Dominici Gregis* on 8 September 1907, the festival
of Our Lady's nativity. Thus, he places the whole controversy about the heresy of modernism under the gaze
of the Immaculate One, who is always interceding for
the Church.

Whatever may have been the encyclical's reception at
the time, it is clear to the honest eye that *Pascendi* cannot be considered a mere doctrinal antique, an artefact
of bygone ecclesial intolerance. Today, the effects of this
synthesis of all heresies are to be met with everywhere.
In a word, theological modernists are those who have
no time for the truly supernatural. Divine Revelation,
grace, Sacred Scripture and Sacred Tradition, liturgy,
the Church herself—all these are displaced and entirely
subjected to anthropocentric concerns.

Again, we have the sad advantage of being able to
mark what happened to Catholic theology, worship, and
culture in the mid twentieth century. The errors of St
Pius X's time have borne their fruit in our own.

As for Our Lady, the saintly pope names her *cuntarum hæresum Interemptrix*[37] the destroyer of all heresies. Does he have precedent for doing so? He does. We find an antiphon in the Roman Breviary which reads, 'Rejoice, Virgin Mary! You alone have brought to ruin all the heresies throughout the world.'[38] We ought to think of the conflict between St Cyril and Nestorius and the resulting orthodox Marian victory at Ephesus.

Here, our purpose is to acknowledge how the sacred liturgy joins together joy and the defeat of theological error. Rightly indeed is Our Lady exhorted to rejoice, for joy only flourishes with the truth.[39]

The point is further proved for us. The psalm to which this antiphon is attached is the 95th: 'Sing to the Lord a new song: sing to the Lord, all the earth... For he shall judge the world in equity, and the people in his truth.' When we study the entire psalm, we see that the modernist could never pray it, because it is precisely the opposite of his joyless doctrine. Modernism pretends to the glorification of man, but has nothing in common with the vigorous simplicity of Psalm 95.

In the end, *all the mysteries of Mary point to the boundlessness of God's ingenuity to save*—which is the very thing that the modernists refuse to see. This is why, in the language of the liturgy, she alone is the destroyer of all heresies. Christ is the Saviour, and this Saviour has a

---

37   Cf *Pascendi*, 59: *adsit prece atque auxilio Virgo immaculata, cunctarum haeresum interemptrix.*
38   Common of Feasts of the Blessed Virgin Mary, Matins, third nocturne: *Gaude, Maria Virgo: cunctas hæreses sola interemisti in universo mundo.*
39   Cf 1 Corinthians 13, 6.

mother. Who more than she is concerned with right understanding of his identity? On the contrary, how entirely foreign to the Catholic sense are the mitigations and insinuations of the modernists!

Rejoice, indeed. And Pope St Pius X knew it: our Lady reminds the Church that joy is true only when it is also faithful.

MEDITATION XI

The Reward Love Looks For

HE SAINTS OFTEN do and say things that leave us rather amazed. For the saints have the grace to see to the bottom of things, and to point out the profound basics of the spiritual life. One saint appears on the brink of Advent and gives us just such a lesson.

St John of the Cross (1542-1591) is commemorated on 24 November. A brief but powerful episode from his life comes down to us. Our Lord and St John are in conversation.

> *Joannes, quid vis pro laboribus?*
> *Domine, pati et contemni pro te.*
> 'John, what would you have in exchange for all these labours of yours?'
> 'Lord, to suffer and be despised for you.'

If we take St John's reply to be nothing more than a manifestation of the masochistic side of religious zealotry, then we will have missed the point entirely.

The astonishing thing is that St John had a desire to suffer as a reward for his labours. Suffering, we ordinarily think, is something that garners a reward;

something we pass through and then receive respite from. On the contrary, St John reveals that there is more to the question than that: suffering borne well unifies the soul with Christ. And that is no invention; it is a truth that runs through the entire doctrine of St Paul.

St John's loving dialogue reminds us of a similar episode from the life of St Thomas Aquinas. When he was asked a similar question by Christ, namely, about the reward he might seek in exchange for his faithful teaching, his answer is like St John's: *Non nisi te*, 'Nothing except You.' And this confirms what we said above. St John knew that sacrificial suffering gives Christ to the soul. Thus, our two holy friars used different words, but asked for the same thing.

And it is St Thomas himself who reminds us that zeal is an effect of love[40].

We do well to note that St John of the Cross occupies a place in the great post-Tridentine Catholic revival. St John is four years old when Martin Luther dies in 1546. And what a story of contrasts! How differently each man engages his suffering before God, how different their fruits. And the contrast appears all the more starkly when we remember that St John suffered most acutely at the hands of his brethren in religion.

The grace of St John's love of the Cross is fittingly celebrated as Advent begins: for it is during Advent that the labour pains of creation and the struggle of the Church Militant are especially put before us. And

40   Cf *STh* IaIIæ, Q 28, art 4. 'I answer that, Zeal, whatever way we take it, arises from the intensity of love. For it is evident that the more intensely a power tends to anything, the more vigorously it withstands opposition or resistance.'

anyone who has suffered much knows the power of St John's words: *pati et contemni pro te*. Would it be really that presumptuous for us to make them our own?

In Clipeos Aureos

THE TRIUMPH OF THE
IMMACULATE HEART
IN THE LITURGY OF OCTOBER

THE MYSTERY OF THE Blessed Virgin Mary appears variously in Sacred Scripture, like a theme in a symphony.

In early October, the Church's course of sacred reading makes its way to the First Book of Maccabees. A Vespers antiphon for the second Sunday of the month strikes the notes of victory: 'the sun shone upon the shields of gold and the mountains were resplendent with them: and the courage of the nations was put to rout.'[41]

The antiphon is a paraphrase, not a quotation; and it seems to suggest that the shields were those of the Israelites. But the reverse is true, as the biblical text shows in context:

> Now when the sun shone upon the shields of gold and of brass, the mountains glittered therewith: and they shone like lamps of fire. And part of the king's army was distinguished by the

---

41 Antiphon at First Vespers: *Refulsit sol in clipeos aureos et resplenduerunt montes ab eis: et fortitudo gentium dissipata est.*

high mountains, and the other part by the low places . . .[42]

However, it is certainly not unusual for the sacred liturgy to adapt a given text for this or that purpose. Like the facets of a gem, Sacred Scripture can be viewed first from this angle, then from that, without any diminution of its lustre—in fact, to turn the gem in one's hand only increases its brilliance. And so, in this case, the reversal is fitting: though the mountains glittered with the shields of the enemy king, his armies gained no swift and decisive victory over the faithful of Israel.

But these shields of gold call to mind another reference. During an extended description of King Solomon's immense wealth, we read: 'And Solomon made two hundred shields of the purest gold: he allowed six hundred sickles of gold for the plates of one shield.'[43]

These shields are a sign of his own triumph—a triumph, not of arms, however, but of wisdom:

> I myself also am a mortal man, like all others . . . Wherefore I wished, and understanding was given me: and I called upon God, and the spirit of wisdom came upon me. And I preferred her before kingdoms and thrones. . . . Now all good things came to me together with her, and innumerable riches through her hands.[44]

Of course, the Church has always understood the 'she' of holy wisdom to refer also to she who is the Mother of God. Thus, in some way, the glory and

---

42 1 Maccabees 6, 39-40.
43 1 Chronicles 10, 16.
44 Wisdom 7; 1, 7, 8, 11.

mystery of the Virgin shines out through the golden shields of Solomon.

But the Virgin Mary is connected to the images of arms in another part of the sacred liturgy in this latter half of the year. We remember an antiphon from the office of the Assumption: 'You are fair and graceful to behold, Daughter of Jerusalem, terrible as an army set in battle array.'[45]

Hardly inappropriate, then, to see reflections of Our Lady in the power of Israel's ancient military grandeur.

The references may appear somewhat disparate—until we remember that spiritual truths are not communicated by syllogisms alone. Here, in the month of October, the images and associations do hold together. (We note that October 7th is the feast of Our Lady of Victory.) The combination of martial imagery and the mystery of the Virgin Mary amounts to a great sign, a sign that appears in the sky of the sacred liturgy, as well as history itself. St John beheld it when the veil was parted: 'And a great sign appeared in the heaven: A woman clothed with the sun, and the moon under her feet, and on her head a crown of twelve stars.'[46]

October 13th is the anniversary of the Miracle of the Sun at Fatima. The event took place 103 years ago today.

Now, our point here is not to rehearse the events of that day nor to expound the message of Fatima. But the liturgy of October is pointing to the Virgin of Fatima, to the woman who promised a *triumph* of her Heart. And *triumph* is a word distinctly martial in its origin

---

45 *Pulchra es et decora, filia Ierusalem: terribilis ut castrorum acies ordinata.*   46   Revelation 12, 1.

and connotation. Hence, the sun shone with a terrible beauty upon the shields of combat in the days of the Maccabees; and, closer to our time, the same sun danced marvellously over a rain-soaked plain filled with prayer.

The liturgical fittingness of the matter continues. The mystery of Christian combat will appear more clearly in the texts of the breviary and Mass during these autumn months—and this because Advent approaches, the great season of eschatological struggle and reckoning. In our time, which becomes more Maccabean by the day, we cannot afford to miss the matter: for indeed, the golden shields of the heroes of Israel prefigure the glimmering triumph of the Heart of the Immaculate One.

MEDITATION XII

The Law & the Little Way

IN THE PARLANCE of the New Testament, 'the Law' usually indicates the Mosaic Law, and the statutes and customs derived from it. That is to put it most simply. But whatever else could be said about the nature and content of the Law, the point is that it was the object of obedience. In that connection, therefore, attempts to paint Christ as an antinomian fall entirely flat:

> Do not think that I have come to destroy the law, or the prophets. I am not come to destroy, but to fulfil. For amen I say to you, till heaven and earth pass, one jot, or one tittle shall not pass of the law, till all be fulfilled. He therefore that shall break one of these least command-ments, and shall so teach men, shall be called least in the kingdom of heaven[47].

There are other passages in the Gospels and the Epis-tles in which the specific content of the Law is clarified. Nevertheless, it is clear that careful observance of the law is not optional for the Christian, but necessary.

---

47   Matthew 5, 17-19.

But thinking of jots and tittles—that is, of the littlest things—one thinks of the Little Way of the Virgin of Lisieux, St Thérèse of the Child Jesus and of the Holy Face (1873-1897). Her genius was to bring a corrective simplicity to the contortions and low-grade neuroses that so characterise man in the modern period. And it would not be incorrect to say that this genius was founded upon love of the law.

For her Little Way of Trust and Love is, in truth, about faithful observance. All her biographers note that she was meticulous in her religious discipline: and this is especially interesting given that, objectively speaking, the Carmel of Lisieux was possessed of a certain laxity.[48] But her Little Way is the very opposite of a scrupulous, legalistic posture of the spiritual life. She observed the law, but for the entirely correct reason: love.

St Thérèse knew and taught that the smallest acts done out of love become great things because of the merits of Jesus Christ. Thus, her doctrine is entirely consistent with (indeed, is an expression of) the doctrine of St Thomas, who teaches that charity is the form of all the virtues.[49] Which is to say that the purpose and perfection of all the virtues is love; all the virtues are reducible to and expressions of love; all the virtues are lived because of love.

---

48 Cf Ida Friederike Görres, *The Hidden Face: a Study of St Thérèse of Lisieux* (San Francisco: Ignatius Press, 2003), 232ff: 'Even on her deathbed Thérèse was tormented by the thought of all the easy-going negligence of the convent, by the lack of understanding of the meaning of perfect obedience.'
49 *STh* IIa IIæ, Q 23, art 8.

It is in this sense that St Thérèse was a great observer of the law, and why she is fittingly regarded as a doctor of the Church. Frail human nature usually baulks at the challenges of the law and is quick to point out its heaviness. On the other hand, the Little Way is a decisive remedy for our own lazy or legalistic tendencies: for the divine laws are observed because they are expressions of love.

Imagine if, instead of giving the *challenges* of the law the last word, we were more like St Thérèse. Imagine if, like her, when confronted with the demands of the laws of love we said, 'This is the least I can do for God.' Then we would know why those who instruct the many to observe the law will shine forever like the stars of the firmament.[50]

---

50   Cf Daniel 12, 3.

MEDITATION XIII

There is Peace in His Wounds

*I*N CH 20 OF ST JOHN'S Gospel, Christ appears before the barricaded apostles. He bids them peace; they seem to hesitate. He then shows them his Wounds; they rejoice. He repeats his greeting of peace. *Pax vobiscum.* The lesson is clear: there is peace in his Wounds.

One apostle is absent, however: St Thomas.

So the episode is repeated. A week later, again the greeting: *Pax vobiscum.* This time, Our Lord goes directly to St Thomas, and bids him touch the sacred Wounds. Then St Thomas, forever dubbed *The Doubter*, believes. And, in believing, he receives the peace of those Wounds.

And yet perhaps we can reconsider St Thomas' initial hesitance to believe his fellows. We call it doubt, as does the Lord himself: 'cease thy doubting,' he commands. But we do not know why he doubts; perhaps this leaves a little space for speculation. First, we do well to note that St Thomas replies to the initial reports, not with a whole-sale rejection of the possibility of Christ's being alive, but with some conditions: '*Until* I have seen the mark of the nails on his hands, *until* I have put my finger into the mark of the nails, and put my hand in his side...'[51]

Now it is true that supernatural faith is condition-less, in a certain sense. But in this case, why didn't St Thomas simply say something more usual, such as, 'Until I see his face'; or, 'Until I hear his voice'; or, 'Until I am able to embrace him'? He said none of these things, but instead, made reference to the Wounds of Christ. It is the Wounds he needed to see.

Obviously there could be any number of reasons why he speaks this way. But perhaps—and this is the central insight for now—perhaps St Thomas more than all the apostles knew that it is the Wounds of Christ that most define Him. Perhaps it was that St Thomas knew that an un-wounded Redeemer was no redeemer at all. (After all, we know that St Peter had difficulty with the prospect of a suffering Christ, which merited him that startling rebuke![52]) Perhaps St Thomas knew more than the others that the Wounds of Christ were essential. Without His shining Wounds, could it really be the Saviour? The supreme moment of the earthly life of the Messiah was when he received these Wounds. How could He return from the sepulchre without them?

Perhaps St Thomas understood himself enough to know that there could be no peace outside of these Wounds, and for exactly the same reason as Isaiah the prophet had said so long ago: 'by his wounds we were healed.'[53]

So yes, St Thomas can be accused of a certain haughty slowness to believe. But perhaps it is more than that. Our Lord's Wounds bring peace to the apostles,

---

51 John 20, 25. 52 Cf Mt 16, 22. 53 Isaiah 53, 5.

and assurance. The assurance is twofold: first, that Christ's Wounds show Him to be the God-man who can save; second, that there is no such thing as an un-wounded Catholic faith. There is no true religion without wound-giving sacrifices.

And from all that, *we* can derive peace. *Pax vobiscum.* For us, too, those Wounds bring peace—with our own assurance that the wounds we suffer for Him make us, not far from Christ, but certainly very near Him.

Prison Thoughts on the Immaculate One

AN ADVENT SERMON

YOU'LL RECALL THAT I wanted to say something about Our Lady on each Sunday of Advent. For the moment, it seems that I ought to be brief about it this weekend.

But I met someone recently—another priest, actually. I met him through some of his writings, which a kind person recently sent me. This priest's name is Fr Alfred Delp. He was born in 1907 in the southwest of Germany. He enjoyed study, and was good at it, and joined the Jesuits in 1926. He taught in various schools (as one does, being a Jesuit) and was ordained a priest in 1937. He worked on a Jesuit newspaper until it was shut down by the Gestapo in 1941. Then he served in a Munich parish, where he was a dynamic and beloved preacher.

But as you'll recall, an attempt was made to kill Adolf Hitler on 20 July 1944. As a result, hundreds of arrests were made. Fr Delp was one of them. He wasn't directly involved with the plot, of course, but he knew some people who were. So he was kept in solitary confinement, continually handcuffed, in the cold. But with the help of the ingenious ladies who were caring for his laundry, some of his writings were smuggled out of prison—and they are sitting on my desk in the rectory.

On the 8th of December, 1944—the feast of the Immaculate Conception—another priest came to visit him and received Fr Delp's final vows, a thing he had been waiting for with great longing. Later, the Gestapo promised him his freedom if he would renounce these vows—but he refused.

In January, his lawyers got him acquitted of the charges of high treason. But that didn't matter. The war was going badly for the Third Reich, and everybody could see that the likes of Fr Delp stood diametrically opposed to the tottering regime. On 2 February—the Purification of Our Lady—Fr Delp was hanged, at 3:23 in the afternoon. His body was cremated, and the remains scattered over the waste heaps of the city. He was thirty-eight.

So in the end, I would like *him* to say something about Our Lady this weekend. He wrote the following while he was in that cold Berlin prison:

> She is the most comforting figure of Advent. That the angel's message found her heart ready, and the Word became flesh, and in the holy room of her motherly heart the earth grew far beyond its limitations.... That God would become a mother's son and that a woman could walk upon this earth, her body consecrated as a holy temple and tabernacle for God, is truly earth's culmination and the fulfilment of its expectations.[54]

54 Alfred Delp SJ, *Advent of the Heart: Seasonal Sermons and Prison Writings*, trans Abtei St Walburg (San Francisco: Ignatius Press, 2006), 27-28.

Words written through handcuffs. We cannot fail to be amazed that the Maid of Nazareth should be the loving preoccupation of a condemned man. And imagine if we understood them half as much as he who penned them. Imagine if in our moments of difficulty and decision we loved her half as much as he did.

Si Igitur Voluit, Fecit

A HOMILY FOR THE IMMACULATE CONCEPTION

'Ave Maria, gratia plena:
Dominus tecum' (*Luke 1, 28*).

HAS ANOTHER HUMAN being ever been greeted like that? No, indeed: no angel ever called any man or woman 'full of grace', except in this moment which St Luke has faithfully recorded. Do we know what a unique truth we utter each time we say the Hail Mary? Imagine what a remarkable thing it is to say: *'Ave, gratia plena!'*

Today, in order to help us to see what a unique privilege Our Lady received, the Church places her side-by-side with Eve.[55] And it is meant to be a story of contrasts. Both are visited by angels. Eve is met with temptation; Mary receives a mission. Eve in her pride is deceived; Mary in her humility remains faithful. Eve takes what is not hers; Mary receives an unlooked for gift. Eve hides for shame; Mary is clothed in dignity.

---

55 The Roman Breviary reads Genesis 3, 1-15 at the first nocturn of Matins, whereas the reformed liturgy reads the same passage, with the addition of verse 20, for the first lesson at the Mass.

And the Scriptures tell us that Eve became the mother of all the living; yet all her children—from Cain and Abel down to you and me—all her children would live under the burden of her sin. That original sin is the lasting effect and echo of the disobedience of Adam and Eve; a stain, *macula*, which lingers on the souls of every man and woman conceived. Except for one: *Ave, gratia plena: Dominus tecum.*

But how can this be? Fathers and theologians of the Church have long asked the question. If we say that Our Lady was conceived without original sin, does this somehow imply that she did not need to be redeemed by the Cross of her Son? No one ever doubted her unique holiness; but it is a mystery so bright and shining that it is difficult for us to see and consider.

One of the Church's teachers uses a homely image, taken from nature. Eadmer of Canterbury (1060-1124) thinks of the chestnut. It grows inside a casing that is covered in rough spines; but the nut itself has all the beauty and smoothness of porcelain. He writes,

> If God allows the chestnut to be conceived, to grow, and to be formed amid spines without being punctured by them, could he not grant to a human, which he prepared for himself as a temple in which he might dwell bodily and from which he would come forth . . . that though this body be conceived among the spines of sins, it would nevertheless be completely unharmed by their sharp points? He certainly could do it, and he wanted to do it. Therefore, if he wanted to do it, he did it.[56]

---

56   Quoted in *Mary in the Middle Ages: the Blessed Virgin Mary in*

Potuit plane et voluit; si igitur voluit, fecit. Simple but mighty words indeed.[57]

As the collect for today indicates, it was in view of the consummated Passion of Jesus Christ that Mary was preserved from original sin: *in-maculata*, stainless. Like the chestnut that is protected from the spines that surround it, Our Lady was protected by the grace of her Son. Grace went ahead of her, and it is this forerunning grace that we celebrate today. And the more bold and mysterious his works, the more we should love the good God who does them.

Think of the sinless purity of our Lady the next time you see the chestnuts fall in September. And may it never be true of us that we take the power of the Hail Mary for granted.

---

the *Thought of Medieval Latin Theologians*, Luigi Gambero, trans Thomas Buffer (San Francisco: Ignatius Press, 2005), 119.
57   A similar formula will echo in the work of Bl John Duns Scotus.

She Who Makes All Things New

SALVATION HISTORY constitutes a series of renewals. Since the fall of man, Divine Providence has continually intervened to re-fashion man, and indeed, all of creation with him. The various covenants are particular high marks in this process of renewal. The history of the patriarchs, the interventions of the judges, the establishment of the dynasty of King David, the preaching of the prophets, are also prominent examples of God's renewing interventions in the Old Dispensation. With Christ and the establishment of his Church, these interventions become decisive and full.

The Incarnate One took flesh of a Mother; *and in the Blessed Virgin Mary the renewing action of Divine Providence reaches its full intensity.* This is so because the mysteries of Christ's birth, life, and death are inconceivable without her. The Immaculate Conception of the Virgin, her Nativity, the Annunciation, and so forth—all the Marian mysteries are joined in her very person. *Tu gloria Jerusalem; tu lætitia Israel; tu honorificentia populi nostri!* [58]

This explains the spontaneity of true Marian devotion in the Church. *It is a theological instinct*, not a superstitious or idolatrous one.

Therefore, each time a Marian feast comes around—which, thanks be to God, is often—the Catholic people ought to be reminded of the renewing power of grace. Each festival of the Virgin Mary brings with it an especially powerful force and incentive for us to begin again; to take courage, to give ourselves permission to shed whatever depresses the soul. How could it not be so? Because, put in this way, grace is the flourishing presence of God in man, which presence purifies, strengthens, and perfects. Thus we call Our Lady 'Mother of grace.'

---

58   Judith 12, 9.

MEDITATION XV

Concerning Strangeness

THE WORD CONSPIR-*acy theory* is much bandied about today. Not our task to analyse the history, meaning, or fitness of the word. But behind the word rests a real phenomenon to consider, and the phenomenon is this: *people believe that other people believe strange things.* And we should say that by 'strange' we mean the word in its commonest sense: unusual, with a connotation of uncomfortableness.

We may begin by saying that strangeness implies order. We know a thing is strange because it is a departure from a pattern we observe and expect. Already that is important. This implication works against anyone who claims that there are no real patterns of order in the world—or at least no patterns when it comes to human action and identity. But if that were true, human beings could never be strange or do strange things. Yet we all know that they do—that *we* do.

There is a danger lurking, however, an epistemological one. If a given situation appears strange, we may be disinclined to believe what we see or are told. Sometimes, this is good: it is charitable to give the benefit of the doubt to our neighbour, not to be *quick* to believe he is in the wrong or is guilty. It can even be laudable to make excuses for the shortcomings of others. Moreover, it is intellectually humble to suspend judgement, as when we admit that we need more information before the mind can settle upon something.

Yet again, the danger arises when we are committed to *dis*-believe simply *because* of a thing's strangeness. This tendency is a kind of reverse credulity. The credulous person believes too quickly, decides uncritically, is easily deceived. But the person who withholds assent on the sole criterion of strangeness is hardly better off.

The fact of the matter is, un-graced human action *is* strange. When man departs from the natural law and divine law, his actions deviate into the painful, absurd, ugly, and destructive. *This is because human choice and action flourish only when they proceed along lines of order and reason.* And it is fair to say that by 'lines of order and reason' we mean virtue. Furthermore, the Catholic knows what sort of person he is without the divine assistance. Without grace, any sort of deviation is possible; without grace, any sort of harm can be inflicted, and no species of self-serving is off the table.

Those who have been the victims of history's tragedies have had to learn this the hard way. Evil is strange because it is a departure from what is good. Not infrequently, human beings do harbour deviant and disturbing motivations, *do* execute harmful plans—and, if unopposed, achieve their wicked ends.

In Corde Mariæ

ANOTHER SERMON FOR THE IMMACULATE HEART

E STAND ON THE octave day of the Assumption of the Virgin. Fittingly, we commemorate the feast of the Immaculate Heart of Mary, and it is on that collect I would say a few words.

At the centre of today's collect is the word *præparasti.*[59] And it is probably not incorrect to say that all sound Catholic Mariology rests upon this one word. Or at least there are many other words that are important for her mystery—but you cannot go without this one.

Note well that the verb is in the second person singular: 'You have prepared'. We have to say something obvious but important: God is the author of the mysteries of Mary. Neither Pius IX nor XII, nor for that matter Celestine I (at Ephesus), nor St Louis de Montfort, nor St Anselm, nor St Bonaventure, nor St Bernard, nor St John Eudes, nor any other eminent Marian doctor of

---

59 It is nearly at the numerical centre: thirteen words before it and fifteen after.

the Church is the author of the mysteries about which they wrote and taught so eloquently. The Blessed Virgin Mary is the work of *God*.

We admire the work God does in Our Lady, and we are moved in the same instant to praise and thank Him, which is exactly what the prayer says today: *contemplating her Heart, O Lord, give us to flourish in your Heart*. The Hearts of Jesus and Mary are two different entities, it is true—but they are so united in grace and purpose, that to see one is to see the other. Mary is not a god; but she is the true God's highest work. Bl Ildephonse Schuster says it—

> Mary is the Creator's finest work. When, in Holy Scripture, we read the praises of the Spouse in the Canticles, of sacred wisdom, of the Church, these praises must be applied to Mary first and foremost, because she embodies in the highest degree the holiness and perfection which is attributed to the mystical Spouse of Christ—the Church.[60]

So we do that today. *We have a loving duty to be enthralled with the Marian mysteries*, because our admiration will lead us to love. In St Mark's Gospel we hear how the crowds admired Christ for his healing and teaching. *Bene omnia fecit*, they said.[61] 'He did all things well.' And in the Heart of Our Lady, he most certainly has.

---

60 Ildephonse Schuster, *The Sacramentary*, vol V (Waterloo, Ontario: Arouca Press, 2020), 67.   61 Mark 7, 37.

Ingram Content Group UK Ltd.
Milton Keynes UK
UKHW011832040423
419625UK00004B/511